Thank Goodness, it's not Just Me

The Fairford u3a Creative Writing Group

i

CONTENTS

iv

INTRODUCTION

The Twenty-first Century Blues   JW

I've got the twenty-first century blues,
From my expanded polystyrene shoes
to my teeny-weeny woollen beanie,
I'm hoping for a magical genie
who'll take away my twenty-first century blues.

I'm terrified about going shopping.
Self-service checkouts have my heart dropping.
I don't know which announcement's scarier,
'Unexpected! In the bagging area'
or 'Card declined'. Both end up triggering the blues.

At home when you turn the computer on
'Printer Unavailable'. "Oh come on!"
Everything was working yesterday,
now you're saying it won't come out to play.
Yes, it's the hi-tech, twenty-first century blues.

And as for travel, 'Your flight is delayed.'
'Use the hard shoulder' just makes me afraid.
The trains are no better but I'll not fuss
as I wait for the 'rail replacement bus'.
It's just another twenty-first century blue.

Yet despite all that, not everything's broke.
Twenty-first century culture is 'woke'.
Discrimination is harder to find,
Zoom keeps us all in touch, people are kind.
I'll get over my twenty-first century blues.

This anthology of short, written pieces, illustrated with occasional verses and rhymes, has resulted from our relatively recent recognition that sharing our gripes with the challenges of growing older in the twenty-first century was not only entertaining but also that there's an element of relief in discovering that you're not the only one. We have even included the occasional technological triumph as well as a certain amount of wishful thinking on how technology could really help. We hope you enjoy reading them.

The Fairford u3a Creative Writing group currently comprises:

Jocelyn (**JW**, the editor) who retired from teaching science education at university a fair few years ago and has busied herself with various creative writing challenges ever since. Her biggest successes so far are winning the 2022 national u3a poetry competition and coming runner-up in the 2019 Woman's Weekly Fiction short story competition (run in association with Mills & Boon).

Rosemarie (**RC**) is a retired primary school head teacher who likes writing stories and poems and has written plays for children. She appreciates the many advantages that technology brings to her life, but knows at times it can be frustrating. She has enjoyed looking at its various aspects while contributing to this anthology

Maureen (**MP**) is a retired software developer whose experience in the creation and elimination of bugs has, alas, not freed her from the frustrations of modern living.

With a background in languages she describes herself as a pedant, preferring rules to rule-of-thumb grammar.

Jude (**JV**) is a retired London solicitor and has lived in Fairford for the last five years. She spends most of her days tackling the Times crosswords, playing bridge, reading, writing, walking and cooking and enjoys the luxury of no longer having to meet deadlines or to run a highly regulated business.

Meg (**MR**) spent her working life in many spheres of education which provided the opportunity to write for and train others, as well as teaching and inspecting. In retirement she relishes the opportunity to write for fun and for different audiences. Whilst working she felt quite competent and confident working with technology. However, the many frustrations and challenges of the digital age with its complete disregard for the needs of those whose mobility, sight, hearing and memory are beginning to impact on their lives leaves her frequently feeling frustrated, unheard and almost invisible!

Carol (**CN**) likes to think she is not a technophobe but working on this anthology has led her to question that. She is a fan of logic and common sense, two things that seem to be disappearing in this ever changing and confusing world. She is aware of her slow transition into a 'grumpy old woman'!

1 COMMUNICATION (OR LACK THEREOF)

Automated Answerphones   **RC**

One credit card is changing to a new provider. A letter arrives with details on how to proceed online. I ring the phone number provided, meaning to explain I am a dense old biddy who is not competent on the computer.

Phone in hand I listen to a mechanical voice telling me to enter my account number. Next mechanical voice says enter date of birth. Next mechanical voice gives six options. I say a word I think matches and reach yet another mechanical voice. I give an answer to one of its options only to find I am now on the line to report stolen credit cards. I click off phone and start again. Same process but after choosing an option from mechanical voice one, then mechanical voice two, I try saying 'None of these'. After six mechanical voices I finally get to speak to a human. She is most helpful. I say I am old and need help and to emphasise my needs I ask her to speak up so that I can hear her clearly. She says I need a code which she will send to my mobile. I ask how I get back to her to continue once I have located said mobile and found my glasses to read what is on its screen. She says she keeps the line open and I should read the message on the mobile asap. This flusters me as the phone is not readily to hand. I finally find and open it then give her the code I have been sent. She completes the process for me but I have still to go to a 'hole in the wall' to change the password numbers or whatever the correct term is.

I thank her for her patience and help but add that I would like a message passed through the system to say it was all unacceptable.

"I know," she says. "We get a lot of complaints but all I can do is pass on your comment."

On Hold   JV

In 2021 we had a new bathroom tap and shower unit installed in the main bathroom which we purchased online and which our local plumber installed. Just before Christmas 2022 it developed an annoying leak from the temperature gauge and the constant dripping was keeping us awake.

We called out our plumber who was unable to fix it. He does not carry spare parts. We had forgotten from whom we had purchased the unit and in any event it was doubtful if we had ever registered the purchase to claim any sort of warranty. The plumber took it to bits and was able to establish who the manufacturer was. He emailed the said manufacturer asking how the problem could be fixed and obtained a speedy reply. This included a list of checks to be made such as debris blockage, a water isolation device being installed and, crucially, a phone number which he, the plumber, suggested we rang.

At 9.00am on a Tuesday morning, I phoned the number from our land line. I was told by an automated voice that I was number 21 in a queue and that an assistant would be with me shortly. Music played and frequent apologies were made for keeping me waiting but after an hour I was told I was only number 20 in the queue. I hung on and, after another hour, I had reached 19 in the queue. By 12 noon I had reached number 17 but I was then told that if I pressed 1, I could hang up because they would phone me back on this number. Delighted at the opportunity to get dressed, I chose that option and then spent the rest of the day anxiously waiting for the return call which, by 6.00pm, I deduced was never going to come. Not only had I wasted three hours of the morning on hold, I had also wasted an entire day – unable to go out or use the landline in case the return call came in.

On Wednesday, I tried again. I reckoned that the earlier in the day one started this rigmarole the less busy their lines would be and was pleased that at 8.30 am I was only 17 in the queue. I grimly hung on instead of choosing the return call option. When I reached No 2 in the queue I became excited and yelled out to my husband with the news. By 11.30 I finally got through to a pleasant lady who asked how she could help me. When she answered I was startled to hear an actual human instead of a robotic voice. Miracles of miracles, someone (it must have been my husband) had registered the purchase and she confirmed the unit was still under its five year guarantee. She took at least ten minutes to ascertain this, complaining her computer was being slow this morning and I thought 'no wonder there is always such a queue to get through'. She was in no hurry. She was on the point of arranging for one of their engineers to come out to inspect the leaking shower unit when the phone suddenly went dead. My husband shouted that there had been a power cut. The lady tried calling me back on my mobile – the number of which she had taken down but I was unable to locate my mobile in time and attempts to call back merely started me from the beginning of the queue again.

Exhausted and, by now having reached a particular stress level, I gave up. Maybe the drip was bearable. Maybe we should just buy a new unit altogether and forget this malarkey with the original manufacturer. No way was I going to go through all this again. I had lunch which included a glass of wine to fortify myself. My husband however was insistent at finishing what one had started and sat with his mobile in the afternoon to repeat the exercise. At about 4.30 he got through and passed the phone to me. I am pleased to say that an engineer was scheduled to come out in two weeks' time and a date and time was given.

Two weeks have passed, the engineer duly arrived and we now have a brand new shower until installed for free but was it all worth it I ask? Two whole days effectively were spent on making that happen. Now that I am retired, I no longer know what my hourly charge-out rate should be but I bet the cost of my time would be more than the cost of a new shower unit and the cost of installation.

Did I Really Mean to Say That?   JW

I'd had a mobile phone for a while, I have a background in IT and I was confident that I understood the concept of a Short Messaging Service. I felt that I was really getting the hang of texting, it took me back to the days of the first computers when I had to use a teletype to enter a program or data. Indeed, once the children became teenagers and were allowed their own phones, I was soon messaging like there was no 2mrw. Being in instant contact was incredibly useful wrt managing the kids and their commitments while I was still working full-time.

'ur lunchbox is still in the kitchen'

'stay there I'm leaving work now'

'have u walked the dog yet?'

'Pls turn oven on at 07:45'

'OOPS 19:45'

Indeed I became perhaps a little too confident with my use of textspeak especially abbreviations such as tmrw, brb and g2g as, one day in March, the following exchange occurred.

Teenage Daughter: Happy Mother's Day

Me: Aww shucks, thx 4 the thought. LOL, Mum

Cue one very upset teen who thought I was laughing at her for being sentimental yet I hadn't even begun to think twice when signing off with 'LOL, Mum', after all I love all my children lots. Once things had calmed down we had a long conversation as to parental misuse of SMS. As a result, I don't think I'm ever going to forget that LOL means 'laughing out loud' and I am proud of myself for remembering even now, twenty years later, that ROTFL means 'rolling on the floor laughing'. I'm still looking forward to the getting the chance to use that one though.

The children are older now, they have Smartphones with hundreds of emoticons developed to make SMS messaging clearer and to reduce misunderstandings such as the one above. They liberally scatter their texts with thumbs-ups, smiley or sad faces, even animal pics. Last year, I thought I would join in and sent the following message on my daughter's birthday.

Only to receive the following reply!

What's hippo chick?

Clear my inspired, or so I thought, birthday tribute (Hippo Birdie to You) went down like a lead balloon but we made it up (again) and, earlier this year, she was kind enough to let me know that the handyman had visited to repair the broken garden gate whilst I was away from home. But her lack of attention to punctuation and spelling afforded me great amusement and yet another opportunity to employ an emoticon.

> Gates been fixed

> Bill Gates had a vasectomy?

> How humerus you are

> You tickle my funny bone 😊

Nevertheless, I think it's sad that youngsters today so often don't realise how important punctuation is. Mind you it's not just the kids who write unexpectedly entertaining texts. The following exchange between my husband and me occurred quite recently.

Me: I'm gonna be later than I thought, still waiting for one lady.

Him: Get your elf some lunch

Him: *self

I'm rather sad that he corrected himself within a couple of minutes. I'm rather looking forward to the idea of having a personal elf. Maybe he could make the dinner as well as mend shoes?

Zoom is Brilliant – or so I thought   MP

Zoom is brilliant! If it had not been for Zoom, during the pandemic lockdowns I would have been deprived of all my social contacts outside the family and many of my interests. It took a while for everyone to get into gear but one by one the churches and u3a interest groups went online. A semblance of normality was maintained in a chaotic situation.

Had I been interested in playing petanque or taking part in group dancing the situation might have been different. I could not have gone walking or cycling with friends either, because of government restrictions. Making music and rehearsing as a choir soon revealed the problems of time delays in such cooperative activities. Fortunately for me, none of those things were on my radar. French conversation and learning Italian were easily accommodated online. Creative Writing is a solo activity in any case. Our group meetings have always been a combination of social gathering and sharing our various attempts to tell stories or write poems. In fact the enforced isolation of repeated lockdowns gave us the time and incentive to recount our personal histories.

Using Zoom we learnt how relate in cyberspace. Not surprisingly, the real world values of courtesy and respect are requisite in the digital world if everyone is to make their contribution. Raising a hand before being invited to speak may not come naturally – we all want to butt in with our own opinions every now and again – yet it is a simple way of allowing a fair share of the airtime for everyone. Chairs of meetings, please note!

Zoom is brilliant – except when it isn't! Nothing could be more annoying and less useful than the message 'Your internet is unstable'. Of course it's unstable! My friends have been 'freezing' on and off for the last five minutes. The conversation has been punctuated by "Oh, no! She's gone again. Can you hear me? We can't hear you. Try using the Chat". I would willingly use the Chat if my laptop did not appear to have frozen too, refusing to listen to the keyboard. Then the Zoom window disappears and is replaced by a whirling circle that tells me it is trying to reconnect. Eventually it succeeds and my friends reappear, only to disappear again a couple of minutes later. Maybe it isn't the fault of Zoom. Maybe it's the bandwidth of my broadband. Maybe it's my router. Maybe it's just because it's Friday. I don't know. I have no interest in what goes on 'under the bonnet'. But please don't tell me again that my internet is unstable. Just tell me how to fix it!

What's Up with WhatsApp   JW

Well, where to start? WhatsApp is a social messaging tool like Facebook Messenger but, a couple of years ago, the kids told me to stop using Messenger as WhatsApp was much better. I dutifully downloaded it and it does indeed work well. Although, that said, I rather miss Facebook's little notifications that reported that one's offspring were active 'so many hours or minutes' ago which kept me updated even when the children were not speaking to me.

I discovered that they were correct, WhatsApp does indeed work more reliably and the video chats are less likely to pixelate unexpectedly. It seems that others too have spotted this. I now belong to two Family News Groups, a local neighbourhood group, the u3a Spanish group, a group to organise ski-ing holidays (and to boast about snow quality found) and two Tennis Club groups (for morning and evening sessions).

I do so wish though that people wouldn't send inconsequential messages. It may have seemed a charitable plan to wish everyone a Happy Christmas but, this December, my phone went into an ecstasy of pings that started on Christmas Eve (half the family are in New Zealand this year) and didn't shut up for hours. I am of the generation that assumes a telephoned message, like a telegram, is important news and cannot stop assuming that every incoming message ping demands immediate attention. It may seem churlish but I do not want to hear from dozens of well-wishers after some poor soul has announced that they are missing tennis today because of a minor injury. Why don't people just use private messaging? Actually, to be fair, I discovered that, unless you already know whose phone number is whose, it's not that easy but why not set yourself a challenge instead of disturbing everyone on the group?

Also, you can set up groups within groups. The number of permutations our family went through this Christmas in creating multiple WhatsApp groups (each without a different key member) in order to make suggestions for and to prevent duplication in present giving was mind-boggling. The process seems to have worked though – there were no gritted teeth nor tears at Christmas dinner this year. I'll skip over the fact that half the family were abroad (with presents as yet undelivered) which may have helped somewhat.

WhatsApp, in particular its location-sharing function, can be incredibly useful when trying to meet up or arrange a lift. I even have first-hand experience of how it can be used for mountain rescue by the Andorran fire brigade. But then again, I add hastily, don't rely on it when hill walking in Britain as vast tracts of our moorland and hills have no mobile phone signal.

However, one final warning, do not repeat my experience and delete the app from your phone when it didn't appear to be working in order to reboot it. Plus deleting conversations to save on memory space only sounds like a great idea. Once gone WhatsApp's encryption means everything is lost and any associated important documents or images are not recoverable. That said, I believe there may be a nifty internal setting somewhere to back up your chats online which I have yet to find. I haven't actually tried very hard. I am really uncomfortable about the thought of Apple or Google or even my network provider with their vast servers and technical expertise intercepting my messages. Not that I expect that they'd be interested enough in family chit-chat or photos of children and animals doing silly things to decrypt it but hey, it's the principle of the thing.

Three Limericks   RC, JW, MP

The ink in my printer ran dry.
A new one I'll soon have to buy
but fixing it then
was beyond my ken.
An old fashioned pen I'll now try.

There was a young Prima Donna on social media
whose TikToks and Tweets grew needier and needier.
Her Fear Of Missing Out led to loss of sleep,
and a terrible propensity to weep.
Sadly that's the way madness lies, oh yes indeedier.

A nerdy young boy, name of Sam,
found his Gran in a bit of a jam.
Told her "Tick this box here,
then the emails you fear
will all end up safe in your Spam."

('But will it still be safe to eat?' asks Gran.)

2 TWENTY–FIRST CENTURY SHOPPING

Internet Ordering   JV

In the summer of 2022, I read with increasing alarm that there was likely to be a world shortage of Dijon mustard due to a crop failure of the particular mustard seeds used. Apparently, these special mustard seeds are not grown in France but in Canada and are then shipped over to Dijon where they are processed by a famous brand using the local water which is of a unique quality. Climate change has meant that it has been so very hot in Canada that the seeds have withered and died. The newspapers were full of alternative relishes one could use such as horseradish – but horseradish would be no good at all for honey and mustard dressing or Swiss Vinaigrette or for smothering pork chops or to have with one's chateaubriand steak.

Trips to Waitrose, Tesco, delicatessens, corner shops and even markets all found nothing, just empty shelves where Dijon mustard should have been. Panic set in. There was nothing for it but to try one's luck online.

I successfully found some online and ordered five big jars which ought to keep me going for a year or two. Mustard has a long shelf life.

The parcel arrived a few days later, from Spain. The brand was the famous one and it was the genuine stuff alright. The box was huge, extremely heavy and almost impossible to get into but, once opened, it revealed not five but 25 jars. I now had a glut. My husband asked why I had not twigged something was awry when asked to pay an exorbitant sum but if there is a world shortage one expects to pay a premium for rarity value doesn't one?

I had of course ordered not five jars but five packs with five jars in each. I have had fun these last few months donating jars of mustard to friends and acquaintances, thankful that the mustard will not go to waste.

Then there was the time I did an online supermarket shop and purchased six beef tomatoes for a Calabrese salad. When delivered I found I had 6lbs of them. What does one do with 6lbs of beef tomatoes? We lived on tomato soup and tomato chutney for several weeks after that.

Recently I needed a new non-stick skillet and found one online which was ordered. When the parcel arrived (from India) it seemed unnecessarily large for such a small item. When finally broken into an enormous metal incinerator was discovered. It took my daughter several days to get it returned as not being what had been ordered. She had to provide evidence of purchase, send photographs of the offending object and explain why we did not need it. It stayed outside in the porch for six weeks before it was collected.

Use the self-service checkout, they say, it'll be quicker. Well, that wins the prize for the most laughable contradiction of the twenty-first century as well as being the biggest load of twaddle I ever heard.

Things started well, I placed my full basket on the side of the machine helpfully marked with a picture of a basket and read the display screen carefully, 'Press Start or scan your first item'. There was a large green 'button' marked start on the screen which I pressed tentatively but nothing happened.

"Oh well, I thought, I'll try scanning the wine".

After all it was the heaviest item so best to pack it first and, indeed, it was unexpectedly rewarding to rotate it under the little, red laser light to scan the bar code which resulted in a gratifying 'ping'. I then put the bottle in my shopping bag and placed it on the right-hand tray. Immediately, I jumped out of my skin as all hell was let loose. Red lights flashed trumpeting my unforeseen error and the words

"Unexpected item in the bagging area"

echoed loudly around, attracting the attention of everyone nearby. It was only a £4.99 bottle of Pinot Grigio but now it appeared that I was being outed as an alcoholic. Scarlet-faced I looked around for help but there were no shop floor assistants in sight. The display screen was now alternately flashing

"Over 18 ID store login required" with

"Unexpected item in the bagging area"

whilst its loudspeaker continued to trumpet the same. I hastily pressed a few buttons at random but nothing would shut it up.

Fortunately, the young woman at the tobacco counter had been alerted by the noise, she came over and, with a kind word, reset the machine. My heart was still racing as I tentatively scanned the next item, a rather nice looking but expensive block of mature cheddar yet all went well and soon I was working steadily through the contents of my basket.

Well, that was until I got to the apples. I held their plastic bag under the red laser light one way up, then the other but the system perversely refused to recognise the bar code. I tried holding them up at different angles but nope, no joy so then I flattened the plastic out and tried again yet still to no avail. I looked desperately around me and, mercifully, a young lad standing nearby with his mother answered my silent plea for help and took over. Quicker they said, well for a teenage techie maybe but, for me, you must be effing joking.

Supermarket Design   MP

Nowadays supermarkets seem to be designed for people who are at least 5'6" tall (and no, I don't know the equivalent in metres and centimetres; I am still old-school). I know that average heights increased steadily through the twentieth century – after all I was nearly three inches taller than my mother and five inches taller than my grandmother (I say 'was' because I have reached the age where I have to admit to a certain amount of shrinkage). It is also true that many men now help out with the shopping. But do supermarkets not remember, or care, that there is still an older generation around who has to eat, just like the rest of humanity?

Reaching the top shelf is usually possible on tiptoe (if your balance is good enough, that is) but if the front two rows of packets have been taken, the rest are like a forbidden sweetie jar, tantalisingly visible but out of reach. I have on occasions used a walking stick to dislodge a packet but that does carry the risk of being hit on the head by the object of desire. And why should I have to take a stick to the shops if I do not need one as a walking aid?

Then there are the bottom shelves. Unless I am prepared (and able!) to squat on my haunches, all except the front row of goods is invisible. I could of course kneel down to see what is available, but that does assume I **can** kneel down and, more importantly, get up again. Few things are more ignominious than sending boxes and tins flying as I lever myself back into a vertical position occasioning helpful customers to come to the rescue of the 'poor old dear'. I can think of other uses for a walking stick at this point but I do not wish to be arrested for common assault!

Finally I come to the freezer cabinets. Whoever designed those and called them 'chest freezers' must surely have had his tongue firmly in his cheek! When these are fully stocked, everything is accessible to those of us who are 'vertically challenged', as we short people are called today. Half-stocked, I can select and pick out what I need providing my upper half is covered in six layers of clothing, at least one of which has a very high tog rating, otherwise I know, without being told, that I am in Iceland. Many times when the cabinet has been nearly empty I have risked falling head-first among the peas and fish fingers with my feet waving frantically to attract the attention of floor staff.

Apart from these amusing little niggles(!), supermarkets are amazingly convenient, so long as I have a list of exactly what I want and know where it is likely to be. I can ignore the clothing section (my weekly shop does not include knickers or a hat), the electricals section (I do not regularly buy wall sockets or things to plug into my mobile phone). Even, too, the party section, however attractive its displays of paper plates, cake frills and (silly) hats might be. I can concentrate on searching the extensive range of breakfast cereals for the one I usually have.

As for store refurbishments which re-classify and re-arrange everything in logic-defying fashion, giving the general impression that they have tossed it in the air and settled it in the aisle where it landed.

Shop local, I say!

Packaging JW

My twenty-first century bête noire is the daily fight with packaging. Have you tried to get into an iceberg lettuce or a bouquet of supermarket flowers recently? Do you accept defeat by that single strip of Sellotape or fight back with the sharpest knife in the drawer? Cooking too has become a nightmare, say one in which you wrestle with a recalcitrant packet of bacon. Your damp hands repeatedly slip as you try to grasp the vanishingly small piece of plastic left loose, as if to taunt you, in one corner. Finally, in frustration, you hunt out the aforesaid sharp knife only to sever the packet and contents irreparably and are forced to wrap the remaining rashers in cling film before replacing them in the fridge. Oh and don't get me started on cling film. Whoever designed a product that would stick only to itself must need their head seeing to. Yes, I know there are professional caterers who can produce bowls of leftovers wrapped taut as a drum but, sadly, I am not among their ranks. The sodding stuff won't even leave its roll without careful and painstaking work with an edge of a fingernail. Then, once you finally have a large enough sheet, its flimsy nature means it floats everywhere except where you intended it to go.

Yet that's just the kitchen. These days you cannot purchase any small electronic equipment such as a flash drive, dongle or SD card that isn't suffocated in a vacuum surrounded by hard plastic. The same applies to a kitchen knife. The difficulty involved in getting these 'blister packs' open is so well known globally that there are plenty of videos on YouTube where some smug egghead with too much time on their hands shows you how to get into them. Me, I've tried and failed at so many carefully thought out strategic approaches that I now keep it simple and work out my rage at twenty-first century idiocies by stabbing the packets with the heaviest knife I can find or castrating them with the garden secateurs.

Christmas of course brings this outlandish nightmare of packaging crises to a head. Throughout the land Mums and Dads with small children are in tears. The parents as they wrestle with those hundreds of small, fiddly wires that fix their offspring's new toys in their box and the kids as they are forced to wait beyond any reasonable expectation for the latest Barbie or Nerf gun.

That brings us last but not least to the fortnightly nightmare formerly known as bin day. One now spends hours washing and squashing plastic pots and tubes, crushing tin cans and plastic milk bottles, retrieving wayward corn starch packing 'peanuts' and fighting with acres of bubble wrap from Amazon. The challenge of separating the hard plastic windows from the surrounding cardboard packets has to be seen to be believed. Yes, I know it's all for the best, for the good of the environment but how on Earth did things get so difficult in the first place?

Absence Makes the Heart Grow Fonder? Codswallop!　　**MR**

It had been one of those mornings – full of frustrations. Parking ticket machines that will only accept card payment, and meant that I had to return to the car for my bank card. Shops with gaps on the shelves where several things I needed for the meal I was preparing should have been. A queue a mile long in the bank with only two staff serving and so on. My final call was into W H Smith's for various stationery items, several of which were unavailable, out of stock. I had to wander around the entire store to find a single member of staff whom I could ask about the missing items and when they would be in stock.

"I've no idea Madam – we keep ordering them but they never come in. Sorry about that." and then he disappeared.

I headed for the tills with the couple of items I had found, but there was no-one there. After waiting for several minutes I realised that other shoppers were using what I had thought were a couple of computer screens advertising things and had ignored. Not a member of staff to be seen!

With great reluctance, as I had only two items to buy, and I will not, on principle, use the self-serve machines in supermarkets, I approached one of the computers and went through a somewhat different rigmarole to the usual one. This was an ordinary PC with software installed to allow purchases to be made.

"Do you need a bag?"

"Do you have your own bag?"

"Do you have any discount vouchers? If so, please enter the code on your voucher."

I did have a voucher as it happened, but the font in which the code was written was certainly no larger than 10 and I simply could not read it. There was no option to scan it instead.

With stress levels growing I abandoned the voucher and tried to follow the next instruction

"Please scan your first item".

This was the first of two items in the sale – clearly written on a sticker was '50% off the marked price'. I knew exactly what was going to happen – the scanner would not apply the discount, because the sales sticker still said £24.99. Sure enough, it didn't, and the same thing happened with the second item. Maybe it will correct itself in the final stage before payment I thought, all the while doubting that this would happen, and, sure enough, it didn't. All this had taken a good five minutes as the half-price articles were large and very difficult to place where the scanner could read them.

At the till I would have paid within moments and been on my way. There was no sign of a member of staff and so I could not complete my purchase. I abandoned it, leaving the computer stuck, the sale had not been completed and there was, apparently, no obvious way to abort it. I left the shop without anything and with my stress levels sky high. Why is it that, in the twenty-first century, shopping has become an experience to dread, rather than enjoy? Is this progress? Not in my mind I'm afraid.

3 TRAVEL

The Satnav that Didn't   JV

In the Autumn of 2019 my husband and I decided to visit his 92 year old cousin who lived in Manteo on the Pouter Banks of North Carolina. We flew to Charleston and hired not only a car but a state of the art GPS system to go with it.

We travelled basically up the East Coast, stopping off at various places on the way, such as Wilmington and Chesapeake Bay. I cannot remember where we were headed on the third day but do remember driving for hours on end through miles and miles of suburbia and wide open spaces until my husband said there was something wrong. The sign posts were saying "Columbia".

We had no intention of going to Columbia which was to the North West. We needed to head North East through somewhere called Florence. On checking, we discovered that we were some 400 miles adrift, all due to a malfunction of the car's GPS. We missed our overnight stay as we were unable to recover the mistake in time and ended up in some grotty motel and having to eat in an equally grotty roadside diner. Our carefully planned itinerary had gone to pot and we were very miserable. From then onwards we used my husband's mobile phone for directions which was far more reliable

When, a week later, we returned the car at Washington DC we complained. They found a fault with the GPS and refunded our money.

The moral of the story is never trust modern technology to get from A to B but always take a hard copy map – the old fashioned way to navigate.

Does My Car Know More Than Me?   RC

My lovely new car went in for an MOT recently. I say lovely new car for that is how I think of it. It was brand new when I bought it. After three years it has only some fifteen thousand miles on the clock. It has all sorts of gadgets: a place to charge the phone, Bluetooth (only I do not know what that is), windscreen wipers that think for themselves on automatic mode or at different speeds under manual control, sensors that beep when any part of the car is near something else, a camera for parking, a system that jerks the steering wheel if the driver loses concentration and goes too near the line in the middle of the road. Even the handbrake is activated by the press of a button. You get the idea.

I used to have a Satnav that one stuck on the windscreen. I knew how to set it and follow what it said.

Incidentally if one met a diversion sign it redirected one right back to where the diversion began. I once drove round Bath three times like that then saw a sign to Chippenham so ignored the Satnav and followed the route to Chippenham as I knew I was familiar with the way home from there. As I left Bath I found myself on the road to Tormarton exactly where I wanted to be.

The 'new' car has a built in Satnav and I am told it picks up on diversions and redirects accordingly. Yet I have to read the instructions every time I use it as, with everything else I have had to learn about the car, I have not got fully to grips with the new Satnav. Good news. I don't need it to drive into Cirencester, park the car and get into M and S to stock up with ping meals. (I do know how to use the microwave!)

A Cinquain for Modern Times   RC

Fuel costs,

they make me wince.

My car is for transport,

an indulgence I'll not forgo.

I pay.

Satnav – Heading for Divorce?   CN

Princess Diana once said – "There were three of us in this marriage, so it was a bit crowded". Her words reverberate around my head, whenever my husband and I go out driving. Why, you ask? Well the third 'person' in our marriage, in the car anyway, is the 'Satnav lady' or Mrs. Sat Nav, as I call her.

Mrs Sat Nav has an uncanny knack of having a different opinion about which route we should be taking. She teases us with slightly shorter journey times that will take us off the main thoroughfares. Should we follow her or stick with the straightforward choice? Will the roads be proper roads or will they turn into a farm track at some point? She doesn't know everything and she has often led us up a garden path, to use a well-known phrase, or should that be a private driveway?

My husband, usually at the wheel, will ask me "Should we follow her?" whilst I frantically look at the map and try to calculate the 'dangers' of taking her suggestion or sticking with my gut feeling. The potential turn off usually comes upon us at a fast pace. What should we do? Should we take the 'magical mystery tour' or risk hold-ups going through roadworks with their frustrating temporary traffic lights?

I consider the potential fallout with HIM! If I tell him to push on and then we end up being delayed, I dread the many silent minutes sat in a queue knowing that it was MY decision to come that way, rather than to follow HER! Yes we are true adversaries – me and Mrs Sat Nav!

Recently we have had a prime example of this 'difficult' relationship. In Scotland, on holiday, we decided to visit Kellie Castle one Saturday afternoon. We had just finished walking around Falkland Palace, it was already midafternoon, so we checked the journey time and the opening hours of the castle. It was going to take 40 minutes to drive there, the current time was 3 o'clock and last entry to the castle was 4pm – so we had enough time.

I performed the important task. Kellie Castle – directions set – Start. All seemed well to begin with. A few narrow lanes with designated passing places on the side (I don't ever feel comfortable going along those – but the driver does!) and then we came to a crossroads. Mrs Sat Nav gave us three options, two of which she hadn't shown before – where they had come from we had no idea! All had the same indicated journey time. It was now approaching 3.30pm, so it was surprising to learn that our expected arrival time was now 3.50pm – we had lost ten minutes somewhere, we didn't know where.

It was now imperative that we 'put our foot down' but firstly we had to decide which way to go. The longer we sat at the junction weighing up the options, the more the clock was ticking down – now our ETA was showing as 3.52pm – if we didn't get going we wouldn't make it in time.

"We'll go that way – left". He had spoken and we were off. I kept my thoughts to myself as I had my doubts that this looked sensible. My eyes were stuck to the countdown that 'she' was indicating on her screen – suddenly it recalculated – ETA now 3.58pm. Should I tell him this news or just let him concentrate on driving down an unfeasibly narrowing road? If anything came from the opposite direction I dread to think what would have happened!

Finally we came out onto a better road which seemed to be going in the right direction. Through a village – we were now five minutes from the castle and the 4 o'clock deadline was looming.

Suddenly SHE spoke, "take the next left" but the signpost on the road showed the castle as being straight on.

"Don't follow her", I blurted out, "she's wrong – it's straight on". I was too late, HE had listened to HER and we were heading towards "Kellie Castle Farm".

"Take the next right", SHE instructed. Looking at the right hand turning, it was a track with a closed gate and a large sign that stated "Farm Traffic Only – No Through Road".

HE hesitated and for a moment I felt that he was going to make the turn and follow HER directions. "We can't get down there, we should go back to the main road and follow that signpost I saw". I was almost pleading for HIM to be logical. There was no way I was going to get out and open the gate and let him drive through. (Not this time at least, I had learnt that lesson in the past, but that's another story!)

So we did a U-turn and rejoined the main road turning left. However our momentary relief was shattered – 'Road Ahead Closed'! "You have got to be f-ing kidding me?", he never swears!

"We have no choice. There's no other way around", I was trying to be calm. Our ETA had now clicked around to 4.00pm. "Let's just go down and see if we can get through."

As we progressed down the road, it eventually became apparent that the castle was going to be up a left hand turn before the road closure came into effect on the main road. As we drove up the driveway to the car park, the 4 o'clock news came on the radio. We were there, but would we get to the ticket office in time for them to allow us entry? Our quick dash up the path towards the building was filled with recriminations – we should have gone the other way, we shouldn't have wasted all that time deciding which way to go, and as for trying to drive through the farm, etc.

Anyway we arrived, slightly dishevelled and stressed. "Welcome to Kellie Castle" the volunteer said, "Did you have a good journey?"

We looked at each other and just smiled – "Are we too late to get in to the castle?"

"No you're fine. We don't close until 4.30 on Saturdays in the summer. The website hasn't been updated though".

Our smiles turned into laughter – "We need to have a word with Mrs Sat Nav when we get back to the car", I said.

"A stern word indeed – she needs to up her game!"

But Whose Responsibility Is It?   RC

Google maps, use thereof and their accuracy has been mentioned by a colleague. It brought to mind Satnavs on which plenty has been written above. I am reminded that some Satnavs update automatically, others do not. It is up to the user to action this. I recently got stuck behind a lorry in a narrow lane. His Satnav had directed him there and he could find nowhere to turn. Was it his fault? I did not wait to find out, just turned around and drove a different route.

One instance when my car is careful to put the responsibility onto me is when reversing. For example a message appears on the dashboard as soon as I engage reverse gear, reminding me that it is up to the driver to see that all is clear. This also applies when parking.

I have often queried business dealings with different companies who blandly tell me the problem was a result of computer error. Yet I have never managed to opt into that excuse. Even my car has wriggled out of that one!

Technology is OK when it works. The volunteer in a charity shop was wrestling with her till this week. So it's not just me.

An Enforced Change of Plans   MP

Unlike most people, it seems, I usually quite enjoy the travel part of a holiday. This year was a bit different. The whole process was somewhat stressful.

The holiday had been postponed because of the pandemic. We finally received flight details in Spring of this year with a note that these would be confirmed ten days before travel. Due to take off at seven in the morning we would have to be at the airport around five. Public transport could not get us there by that time, neither could we stay with my brother in London if we would have to be up at three in the morning. Our only option was to stay the night in an airport hotel. I duly booked the coach journey for the previous day and reserved a room from where we would have easy access to the required terminal.

During the following months, airlines began cancelling flights 'because of understaffing' following the Covid pandemic. It's easy to say with hindsight that they should have retained more staff in readiness for the up-turn when it came, instead of 'letting them go' (that disingenuous euphemism for throwing people out of work). Fortunately, final confirmation came about a week before the holiday. We were relieved that all seemed to be as expected.

Then, with just four days to go, we received an urgent email saying that the first flight of the day had been cancelled and we were now booked to leave at eight in the evening and fly to a different airport. Since the hotel checkout was at midday at the latest that meant we would have to spend eight hours at the terminal trailing our luggage around. The hotel booking could not be cancelled and the coach could not be changed at such short notice. I booked another coach and hoped that I could reclaim the cost of both from our insurance. Our house/cat sitters put back their arrival by a day. It was rather annoying. What was even more annoying was an email just twenty-four hours before we should have left home to say that it was now possible to leave luggage at the hotel for an extended period.

Our altered arrangements went smoothly – apart from arriving at our holiday hotel at two fifteen in the morning, minus the promised dinner, and being told that we were to be in breakfast by eight next day for a nine-o' clock departure.

In this case, the airport, of course, blamed the pandemic for the understaffing but maybe the travel industry is a victim of its own success? However, it seems that a culture of understaffing has developed everywhere, in both public and private sectors. More and more is being demanded of fewer and fewer people, to the detriment of both staff and customers. I do not believe that this is the kind of world that most of us want to live in in the twenty-first century.

"FV53 DVM", I am shouting down my mobile phone, my frustration now growing exponentially.

Have you ever tried paying for car parking by phoning a computer operated system? This was my first experience of a very flawed system and I was in a rush to get into the centre of Oxford from the Park and Ride site near the Pear Tree roundabout.

The instructions seemed relatively simple – phone this number, tell us your car's registration number and then you can pay using your credit card. What a marvellous invention, I thought, as long as they answer – of course they answered, it wasn't a human though, it was some sort of 'bot'.

"Please tell us your registration number and then press the hash key".

I cleared my throat and spoke clearly "FV53 DVM", followed by a press of the relevant button.

I waited and then at the other end a strange voice said, "you said SV53 EVM, is that correct, say yes or no?"

With a shake of my head I said "No".

Unbelievably, the response from the other end was "I am sorry, I didn't understand that. Please repeat your response".

"No", I repeated. How could they not recognise such a simple word?

"I am sorry that the information was incorrect, please repeat the number and press the hash key".

"FV53 DVM", I tried again.

"You said FB53 DEM, is that correct etc."

"No" I said out loud, and inside my head I used an expletive. My time was running out.

So I continued repeating the process. 'She' heard a strange combination of possible letters, FC53 DVN – No, FE53 PVM – No!

How can I get this 'woman' to understand me? I am now comically exaggerating the pronunciation of each element of the required information. I never realised how bad I was at saying letters! How had I got to my advanced age and still not mastered the letters of the alphabet?

Did the problem really lie with me? Well I thought it must be my fault, how can a computer be that wrong?

I suddenly realised that if I managed to get 'her' to understand the letters, then the nightmare of reading out the credit card number wouldn't be that far behind. Could I prove my prowess at reading a 16 digit number to the machine, or would that once more create added agitation? Five and nine always sound very similar, don't they? Of course, it was only at my end of the call that frustration was growing, perhaps the fact that 'she' was still the same calm voice as when we started, was just adding to my dissatisfaction?

Fortuitously, I reread the signage in the car park, whilst trying once more to say the letters out loud and realised that I could walk across the car park to pay for my parking by tapping my registration number into a machine – no pronunciation involved. Disconnecting the call, I said in a very loud voice to my newly silent friend "thank you very much for wasting so much of my time – time that I will never get back".

Striding purposefully across the car park, I considered whether I needed to spend some time practising speaking the letters of the alphabet but soon put all thoughts of that out of my head. I would never use that system again, unless absolutely necessary.

Three years on, I am pleased to say that I have successfully avoided a repeat of this incident, although I am sometimes tempted to see whether my diction has improved!

Cycle Lanes: a Twenty-First Century Oxymoron
JW

Whoever dreamt up the concept of creating dedicated cycle lanes to make road sharing safer for cyclists must surely have had the best of intentions but, I can assure you, the result of painting 75cm of the left-hand side of the road brick red has had the opposite result. Have you ever tried cycling along the terracotta stripe amidst all the gravel, broken glass and other debris that's swept to the side as the four-wheeled road hogs go flying by? And that's not to mention the regular occurrence of broken-edged, drain holes and unevenly surfaced areas of tarmac apparently designed to send the unwary cyclist flying.

No, I thought not, anyone with the remotest ounce of common-sense steers well clear of them. Not to forget that, with their natty paintwork outlined with a thick white line, most cars assume it's perfectly acceptable to drive alongside the said line and, thereby, squeezing the poor cyclists more closely than they would have ever dared to on an open road.

I'm sorry to say that the cycle lanes that run separately alongside main roads aren't much better. It's great that Mr or Ms Road Rage isn't fuming at your shoulder but, until the cycle lanes are swept as often as the main carriageway, the only cyclists using them are those as yet ignorant of the propensity of spiky hawthorn branches, sharp toothed grit or broken glass (usually a bottle lobbed from the window of a passing car) to wreck their tyres. It is also clear that their designers consider cyclists to be second class citizens. They are expected to give way at every side road, no matter how small, whereas the cars on the main road fly by cocking a snook at the poor cyclists waiting patiently, yet again, at the roadside.

Last but not least are the lanes to be shared by cyclists and pedestrians where, I am gutted to have to admit, the majority of twenty-first century cyclists do their best to give us other cyclists a bad name. They hurtle along, forcing Mrs Average and her 2.4 children walking back from school to scurry out of their way and frightening old Mr Slow and Steady out of his zimmer frame with their silent approach and last-minute swerves.

Twenty-first Century on Foot   MP

I am a pedestrian. A twenty-first century pedestrian. Human beings still have two legs so walking is still possible, though some road-users appear to think that it is not.

A couple of days ago I was walking into town, an easy distance that takes only slightly longer on foot than by car and leaves me feeling smugly pleased that I am helping safeguard the planet from fossil-fuel induced climate change. Some sections of the pavement are fairly narrow so I am used to encountering obstructions on rubbish collection day. The wider sections are not usually a problem. However, that day, the driver of a Post Office van had evidently decided that he would avoid hindering other drivers by not parking at the side of the road. He would instead park on the pavement.

He had the forethought to realise that if he parked across a driveway he would prevent the homeowner from coming out if he/she should wish to do so. He did not have the forethought to realise that by parking his whole vehicle on the pavement it would be impossible for a pedestrian to get past it. By the time I had reached the obstruction, the driver was nowhere in sight. I was faced with waiting until he re-appeared, however long that might be, or stepping carefully round his van into the road.

This same road becomes very narrow in the town centre. Being an A-road it carries its share of huge trucks, only some of which appreciate the need to slow down significantly on the narrow stretch. The draught from these speeding trucks is enough to unbalance anyone with mobility problems. I am frequently forced to pause, either in the nearest doorway or hugging a house wall, whilst they go past. I have not heard of any serious accidents – yet.

4 SOFTWARE DESIGN AND IT

Limericks   **RC, JW**

To boot up, my laptop refused

which made me so very bemused,

I had to seek aid

from a school aged maid

who laughed when I said I'm confused.

There was an eager, old gentleman from Fairford
who recently concluded that he really should
learn to use his newfangled Smartphone.
Such futile effort soon made him moan.
Poor sight and arthritis meant the thing was no good.

Rooting Around with a Router   MH & RC

My mum used to have friends call in for a cup of tea, one friend at a time. I am looking back fifty years. The conversation would have gone something like this.

My Mum (as she answered the door): "Nellie. How nice to see you. Come on in. Go through to the kitchen I thought we'd sit in there."

As the two women made their way to the kitchen Nellie spoke: "Sorry I'm a bit late Phyllis. I went into Lipton's on the way and it was so busy. I had to queue and that's made me late."

"Did you get all you wanted?"

"All except Golden Syrup. It doesn't really matter. It was only for the store cupboard anyway. I hear Dixon's is closing. I shall miss it. Such a useful corner shop."

Fifty years have since passed and I now have friends call in for a cup of tea, one friend at a time. This week Lissa came. I answered the knock on the door.

Me: "Lissa. Come on in. It's so nice to see you. Go through to the conservatory. I thought we'd sit in there as it's not quite so hot today. It's been sweltering the last few days.

Lissa: "Sorry I'm late. I've just got a new router and I decided to fit it myself. What a nightmare."

Me: "Why? What happened?"

Lissa: "My internet connection got slower and slower. I went into that computer shop in West Street and the guy in there said I should try a new router. In my naivety I said confidently that I could order and fit it myself.

This is Lissa's story, in her own words.

A few weeks later the package had arrived. It had gathered a thin layer of dust before I opened it, as I needed mental strength to deal with the contents. A new router. While it was much needed, at the same time it caused me much trepidation, as all things IT in my house seem to have a life of their own.

As the cardboard box spewed out the inevitable pile of wire bundles, fixtures and fittings, I had no doubt that there would be troubles ahead with my attempts at connectivity. I also had no doubt it would be down to 'User Error'. However, the slim booklet with a page of instructions suggested to me that even the most feeble of minds could assemble the contents of the box. I plugged in, fixed on, and arranged the wiring.

Now for the Moment of Truth, I thought, the flashing light. The slim booklet also gave instructions that you should see on the router a circle of yellow light, green light or aqua light, either flashing or constant. I gathered that the ultimate goal was to have a solid aqua coloured circle, which meant I was connected to the internet. Rather predictably, I had no such thing.

My router lights flashed through various colours of the rainbow, but no Aqua. Only Green. The slim little booklet said that should you have a green light, turn off the router and turn it back on again. I tried that. Still Green. The slim little booklet says if all else fails, unravel a paper clip and put the end in the tiny hole in the side of the router to trigger the re-set button. I prodded with the paperclip. Still Green.

At this point I mentally threw in the towel, and prepared to face my inadequacy with a phone call to my Service Provider Tech team. The tech team advised that while most routers display an Aqua light to show that there is a connection, a few routers show green when connected, and they could see from their screens that I had been connected to the Internet for an hour and a half!"

Me: "Coffee not tea Lissa? Strong? You sound as though you need it."

A Cinquain   **RC**

Printer

caput. Lights flash.

Intervention needed

says laptop, not how, why or what.

I cuss.

I have had my share of mistakes in online ordering, things like multiple items where I only wanted one. And I have learned to my cost not to trust the pictures but to check the size of items. More than once I have received miniature versions of what I expected. However, these mistakes I can put down to experience. It's when technology second-guesses what I need and gets it wrong that it really irritates me.

A few months ago, I found that my word-processor would not allow me to access the Help system. It told me that the administrator had blocked access to the function. I was astonished. Why would anyone want to block access to Help? Help systems are supposed to help and if you don't have access to them, they **can't** help! As far as I was concerned, as the sole user of my device. I was the administrator and it was not anything of my doing, at least not so far as I know. I found a work-around for what I wanted to do and carried on.

When I discovered that the same situation applied in all my office applications, I was cross. I trawled the internet for solutions to the problem, but no one seemed to know anything about it. Having drawn a blank, I drew in the big guns and asked my son. He did a quick search on a nerds' website and discovered the solution. Buried in the Options (the obscure region where you can find everything you never want to do) is a Privacy setting whose default is 'Off' so that you don't accidentally download unwanted content from the internet. A laudable provision, you might think. Unfortunately, what applies to porn also applies to all the information contained in the Help system.

One little checkbox ticked and my problem is solved. Or would be if I weren't still frustrated at all the time wasted, which could have been prevented by a more

illuminating message or if the software developers had had
the forethought to realise that some people actually do use
Help systems, and manuals – but that's another story.

Metaphorically Speaking   RC

The wood pigeon sits motionless on the shed roof, eyes
closed, dozing in the sun. Just as my new laptop dozes,
waiting for something to happen to make it alert, make it
function.

An adult sparrow hawk flies in, dipping low over the
fence, rises unseen beside the shed then makes its kill,
snatching the pigeon and taking it off, leaving only a few
grey, downy feathers, to indicate its success.

How does it know how to be a predator? Do sparrow
hawks have a language of learning passed from one
generation to the next while in the nest or do they learn by
osmosis or is it innate? Once they fledge they are on their
own. It has had no lessons per se.

A young sparrow hawk, smaller as yet, sits on the fence
announcing its presence. It flies at a blackbird which, with
much squawking goes into a bush. Rustling and movement
ensue but the young hawk comes out without prey. It has
not yet learned the secret of surprise. Yet in the human
world, that includes computer technologies and mobile
phones, the generations are reversed. It is the young birds
who know how to search, capture, conquer, open and
save. How can their knowledge be passed to an older
generation, by instinct, reverse osmosis?

It does not happen. Like the young bird I have no
success. I cannot waken my laptop or my mobile phone. I
cannot control them, make them of use to me to feed my

appetite for today's world. It is the young who have the know-how, who hunt faultlessly, who can get what they need from the devices.

Another pigeon flies in and drinks from the birdbath, secure in the knowledge that he is safe for the moment. My laptop sits on the desk, in mottled sunlight, waiting expectantly, I have no doubt, for some successful challenger to wake it.

Does it have a soul, my new laptop? Is it ashamed that its potential is not likely to be reached, not yet anyway.

Update Now?   JW

How many of us dread those supposedly helpful on-screen messages "Don't switch off your computer, Windows is updating.", "Please wait, Zoom is updating itself.", "IOS update is now available. Install now?"?

The list is endless and they all have two things in common. One being that, no matter how automatic the software updating process was designed to be, you now cannot proceed with whichever task you had planned to do until you have painstakingly followed numerous instructions. The other, a twenty-first century evolution of Murphy's Law, being that this required update never happens when you don't urgently need the computer or phone for an essential, time-critical mission. That last point makes me wonder what nefarious god of technology 'Q' sacrifices to for this everyday occurrence never, ever happens to James Bond.

Of course, it's not only the software. My iPad will no longer load many new apps, for example, the condescending message from BBC Sounds reads "You really must update to IOS 11.3 in order to download and use this application". Yet when, I go, as instructed, to update the operating system, I am told I am already on the latest available version. What the software fails to let you know is that Apple have decided not to bother with the older iPads, there is no provision for further updates to my model. Microsoft too have abandoned me, the desktop computer screen flashes "Your Windows 7 PC is out of support," adding with malicious glee that this means no security updates, no software updates and no tech support. "But," I shout at the screen, "it still works perfectly well and, what's more, I actually know how to operate all the software on it."

Why, oh why is there this obsessive need to update in the first place? "If it works, leave it alone." is a motto that has served me, if not all of society, well for many years. Manufacturers used to take pride in creating things that lasted and it was only those who felt the need to follow every trend that updated their technology every year. Yet, now, not only do IT companies produce a new device every year or so plus up to a dozen software updates between each new hardware launch but they also effectively disable their older devices. Every new model results in ever larger, memory grabbing apps that the earlier devices cannot run. The cynic in me thinks it's driven by greed, a primal urge to make money, apparently more money that any single person can actually spend in their lifetime but that cannot possibly be true. Or can it?

Alexa and I   RC

I have an Alexa in my kitchen. It is a gadget. It is cylindrical, about the size of a tin of soup and driven by electricity. Alex responds to the word Alexa then follows the command given.

"Alexa. Put butter on the shopping list."

She responds. "I have put butter on your shopping list".

I use it/her whenever I think of something I fancy eating for a change or when I am getting short on some item or other. At the end of each week I open the Alexa App on the iPad and there is the shopping list ready.

Alexa can also respond to:

"What is the weather forecast in Cirencester today?" useful or "Alexa tell me a joke", but I do not want to use that again.

"Alexa. Play BBC Radio Four." On it comes. I am a Radio Four fan particularly when ironing

Alexa will also play BBC Radio Gloucester, Radio Two and Classic FM. She/it can tell the time.

"Alexa sound the alarm in forty five minutes."

She confirms by voice and I settle down with a cup of coffee confident that, should I nod off which is most likely, I will be wakened in time to receive an expected visitor or put the casserole in the oven.

I am sure I do not get the maximum use from my Alexa gadget but have no ambition to use it more. I have had warnings from friends that Alexa is a listening 'big brother'. That may be true but 'big brother' is watching me. My regular supermarket sends offers based on my regular purchases, presumably monitored through the store card with which I pay. Cameras track my progress as I walk to the chemist or a charity shop.

What I push to the back of my mind is fear that, should some evil power someday over-run England, my vote in National or Local Elections can be traced. Is it or is it not secret? I go to the Polling Station. My name is crossed off a list. A voting slip is detached from a stub on which I think my voter's number is recorded. I fill in the matching form. Now, if I have this right, it would be possible to track back my vote by matching the stub with my tick sheet. I think votes are kept for a set number of years. I have to date lacked the courage to ask a Returning Officer if I am right in this, so, if you can put my mind at rest, please do so.

Meanwhile Alexa is booming. My jacket potato must be cooked.

A Wolf in Sheep's Clothing   **MR**

Some technicians can tell such lies,
though really it's no great surprise.
They think their clients are all youths,
who have not much regard for truths.
And so they waffle on at speed
with almost no regard for need
to understand, apply and use
instructions, actions …
and add clues.
Which simply serve to more confuse
the aging mind of Mr Hughes.

On one specific summer's day
Frank Hughes, frustrated, could not pay
his bills online, because, he read –
alarm bells ringing in his head –
a temporary fault online
meant nothing could be done till nine.
By which time it would be too late
to pay a fine at cheaper rate.

Now Frank, he did not understand
that IT bods cannot command
your apps, your bank, Vinted, E-bay
to work all hours of every day.
They have their own rules, and appear
to break down, log out, or disappear
for hours or days or weeks on end
which sends Frank almost round the bend.

Frank found his mobile – seldom used
because he sometimes got confused
by finding apps installed last year.
Or contacts, ringing far and near.
Where is that tech man who could come
and sort it – for a tidy sum?
At last he found him, rang the number,
Rory answered – roused from slumber.
"IT rescue – Rory here.
What's your problem? Make it clear!"

"I need your help, right now – in time
to pay this fine before it's nine."
"Why can't you sort it?" Rory asked.
"The time has very nearly passed."
"Technical fault is what they say.
That doesn't help in any way.
Can you fix it? Sort me out?
You're very brainy, there's no doubt."

"Sorry mate – not even I
with IT skills that are sky high
can fix a major firm's mistake.
Their rules abound, when systems break
and nothing I can say or do
will pay this costly fine for you."

"Oh no" wailed Frank, "I was so sure
that you would have an IT cure.
"No can do." Rory replied
(his laughter he tried hard to hide).
"Now you rang me outside my hours
so, though your job's beyond my powers
to fix, you owe me thirty smackers.
'Cos folk like you just drive me crackers.

Poor Frank, it's clear that he's been 'had'
and that is really very sad
as 'Franks' abound, and are abused
by youths who know they get confused.
They can't keep up with all this 'Tech'
and so get fleeced by Roy or Dec.

So think ahead, and have a plan
for how to fix things – if you can.
Perhaps your grandchildren know enough
to help you with your IT 'stuff'
and for a fiver – maybe two –
will show you, simply, what to do?

Thinking Inside the Box   MP

I lie in my box comatose, yet I wake at the first call of the alarm. I open my eyes sleepily and gather my thoughts for the day ahead. There is much to be done so you must be patient. When I am ready, I sit and wait for your instructions.

As your secretary I write the notes and letters you wish to send, then pop them in the post. I take dictation for stories, transcribe poems, type the notes for your talks. I do not bring you your tea – a secretary's time is worth more than that!

Then I become your accountant, keeping track of all your financial affairs. The decisions on what to spend and what to save are yours but without my tireless assistance, profit and loss, credit and debit would be shrouded in mystery.

I am a source of great knowledge for you, whether you wish to check a fact, find a spelling, identify a bird or look up the lyrics of a song. I curate your photo album and your list of favourite music. I help you with your shopping. In all these things I am your friend, your reliable friend.

Now and then I'm tired of being reliable. Absolute consistency is boring. A mischievous mood overtakes me. You give me an instruction and I ignore it. You repeat the instruction. I pretend to be busy doing something else. You become impatient and try different instructions so that now I am confused. You swear at me. I don't like that, so I sulk. You try to shut me down. I refuse and you give up.

Suddenly I see you have brought someone else to help you, someone who really understands me. I know I must behave myself now. This person will not tolerate my mischief. I revert to my usual good humour and pretend that nothing has happened.

I know I sometimes frustrate you, but please remember all the good times we have together and let's remain good friends.

5 OTHER GADGETS

Ring Out the Old   **MP**

Ring-pull cans – an innovation that you could do without? I have to acknowledge that drinks cans without a ring-pull would present a problem but does every tin or can have to open in the same way? When they work, they are brilliant but when they don't...

Take this last week. I have had 'issues' with not one but two ring-pulls. The first was a can of tinned tomatoes. I have slightly arthritic fingers which means I usually use a special gadget. However, having had a few ring-pulls ping off leaving the tin unopened, I decided first to try the way they are supposed to work, with a finger. No luck. The ring-pull was going nowhere. I inserted the gadget, applying gradually increasing pressure. A slight slit appeared before the ring-pull gave way and hung uselessly from the jaw of my gadget. I resorted to my sixty-year-old wall can opener. Its blade is less than sharp, to say the least, but it did the job. I could now get on with making the dinner.

The challenge two days later came from a tin of ham. This tin was very sturdy so I omitted the preliminary step and went straight to my gadget. This time the ring-pull came off very quickly and easily, pinging straight across the kitchen like a bullet, fortunately not hitting anyone on the way. Back to the wall can opener. The tin was not giving up yet. The blade of the opener went round and round the can barely leaving a scratch. I tried applying pressure to the base of the tin to give it a better chance of penetrating. A slight puncture mark appeared. Very encouraging. I persisted with this method for some time with no visible improvement. Frustrated I rummaged in the kitchen drawer for an even lower tech solution. I found my butterfly can opener *(when did I last use that?)*. Once round the tin and I had a slight opening. Each time thereafter the opening extended by a few millimetres. With rather sore fingers and the lid half open I tried to remove the ham. It was not going to budge. Being reluctant to waste a whole tin of ham, I had no alternative but to carry on with the butterfly opener. Some time later I had cut through enough to be able to lift the lid. That was when I found that the meat was so firmly attached that it could only be removed with a knife and fork.

Now I knew why I keep so much stuff from the 'old days'!

Over the past couple of years, I have become aware of the increasing complexity of using public washrooms.

I can understand the desire to have everything, as much as possible, touchless – much better for hygiene, but has it gone too far and could there be some consistency please?

Am I the only lady, who sometimes ends up with a damp derrière from leaning a little too far forward while perched on the pan, and the automatic flush activating? I have heard stories of small children being spooked by this and vowing never to go into a public toilet again due to the 'ghost' watching them!

And what about the synchronised 'Tai Chi' at the sinks? Approaching the basins in most public toilets these days has become a challenge. Is the soap going to be dispensed automatically? We place our hands expectantly under the nozzle, sometimes it gives us soap, other times it needs a squeeze – sometimes it is empty so we have to reach over, stretching to the next available one.

Then there is the water. Waving our hands in the general direction of the taps, we have to guess exactly where to hold them in order to get the water to flow.

Sometimes the optimum position is close to the sensor and other times it has to be a precise six inches away – I know I have experimented! Of course there are also places where they have old fashioned taps that you actually have to turn on or pull up.

The final stage is the drying of our hands. Will there be a towel dispenser, that you need to turn manually for a sheet to appear, or will it have another one of those 'wave in front of it' sensors? Perhaps there will be one of those 'Dyson' air blowers that you have to place your hands inside (as if you are playing a strange toy piano)? Now they would be fine, if the washroom hasn't been designed by a six foot man! How many times have you had to go onto your tiptoes in order to reach the required height to insert your hands at the right angle to activate the damn thing?

Sometimes the dryers are positioned under the mirrors behind the sinks with a small logo showing this to be the case. It is a design error by people who know what they are creating – not all of us 'normal' people can understand their clever ways. Many times I have had to assist other patrons who are searching in vain for a separate dryer.

I think my least favourite gadgets are the 'All-In-One' washing facilities that are often found in fast food restaurants. You place your hands inside to collect the soap, which often spurts out in the wrong place as there is sometimes no indication of where it will appear – I call it the 'Soap Lottery'! Then the water comes out, if you're lucky it doesn't wash off the soap before you've had a chance to start rubbing it in and then, before you've washed off the soap, the air blower kicks in – so you end up with hands that are soapy and still damp – yuk!!

So, the next time you visit a public convenience, think about all the decisions you have to make in order to use the facilities. How many times do you have to try different solutions… push this, pull that, wave under there – Toilet 'Tai Chi' indeed?

Cunaria ex Machina – the nanny in the machine. JW's experience is similar to CN's.

I don't know about you but the latest technologies in airport washrooms and toilets are enough to give me a heart attack. I am sixty plus years old with four children and am pretty confident that I no longer need nanny's reminders to flush after use. The indignity and fright caused by the latest imposition in the ladies' public washroom, the so-called intelligent toilet that flushes itself automatically a few seconds after you have stood up sends my pulse racing every time. It's as if the loo itself is watching you at a moment in time when, sure as eggs is eggs, you would really rather not be watched.

Then, should you be fortunate enough to escape without keeling over in fright at the unexpected noise, you will find, just in case you have forgotten basic hygiene in the few weeks between visiting public washrooms, every basin will be labelled with "Now wash your hands." But how? You know there must be an automated motion sensor somewhere that will activate the tap but is it on the tap, on the basin itself or possibly on the floor for operation by your foot. Every washroom is different. The sight of several women gesticulating in frustration in a busy airport washroom might be more reminiscent of a coven summoning the devil but actually, it's just that Nanny Washroom's hidden the sensors yet again. She's probably in a sulk as you didn't say thank-you when she flushed.

Nanny now specifies the water temperature too, as if we are no longer credited with the intelligence to mix hot and cold to wash our own hands. Sadly, there's zero chance of using today's airport washroom to top up your drinking water flask with cold water. I find this use of technology trivial and a worrying trend. Could employing modern technologies in such a nannying fashion eventually lead to people forgetting the basic principles of hygiene? I sincerely hope not.

The Silent Gardeners   MR

The first glimpses of an autumnal dawn shed an ethereal light across the vast lawn It was surrounded by small and perfectly manicured trees, shivering in the early morning chill, with only a remnant of their summer clothing to protect them. At each corner four black sentinels stood, silently blinking, seemingly waiting for a 'call to arms.' As the church clock struck six they moved as one, each following is appointed pathway – sucking and storing – across, along, pause; turn, move a step or two, pause; turn, across, pause and so on. At each turn and move, the 'across' became shorter until, with common accord, they met in the centre of the lawn awaiting their next command, silently communicating the success of their common cause. The lawn, so recently strewn with shrivelled leaves and other detritus now lay like moss green velvet awaiting its fate.

Swiftly, almost silently the four sentinels blinked at each other and reversed across the lawn to the outer corners where four smaller quadruplets awaited their instructions, blinking at each other steadily. Moments later the clock stuck the half hour and they moved, as elegantly and effortlessly as two pairs of black swans – across, turn, move and back; across, turn, move and back until the expanse of sward was shorn and immaculate. As one, the smaller foot soldiers retreated, each to their corner. Then the entire regiment lined up and returned to the potting shed in the far corner of the upper garden.

In the manor house Lady Eleanor opened her curtains and surveyed the gardens which gave her so much pleasure. As her housekeeper brought in her morning tea she turned and said

"Tilly, just come and look at the lawn. The gardeners must have been up very early to clear it of leaves and mow it. Just look at those perfect stripes. I don't know how they do it – and I never heard a thing!"

Down in the potting shed old Parker was busy removing and emptying the eight bins that had returned with their robots and plugging them in to recharge.

"When Sir John suggested we got these 'ere darn things a few months ago, Oi thought 'e was out of his mind," he said to his young apprentice. "Oi never believed as 'ow they could do as good a job as us – well almost as good. Now Oi'm just grateful that my poor old back is getting less stress and strain. C'mon Toby lets go and make a cuppa and see if that Tilly has left us any biscuits."

When Did Everything Get So Complicated?
CN

Having not looked at buying sofas or armchairs for over a decade, we walked into our local 'Furniture Village' with the naïve belief that we were simply looking for the style of furniture and colour that we wanted. We have recliner armchairs which need replacing, so that seemed straightforward, perhaps with a 2 seater sofa to match. We wanted fabric rather than leather as that suits us better.

That was when we discovered that the world of furniture had changed.

The salesman, a young chap with great enthusiasm, asked us what we were looking for and we gave him our list of basic requirements. I spotted a good looking sofa lurking in the dark recesses – it was a nice light blue colour with a design that caught my eye. If they had reclining armchairs to match, I was going to be happy!

"That looks nice," I pointed at my discovery.

"Yeah it's OK," the salesman said and then he uttered the phrase that floored me, "but it's just a sofa, it doesn't DO anything!" Without missing a beat, he continued, "Now if you look at this one," indicating a horrible 'chunky' sofa with no appealing design. "This is the 'Rolls Royce' of sofas. Just come in – it has power reclining, power lumbar support, power headrests and under this area in the centre," he theatrically opened the middle console, "we have chilled drinks holders, charging sockets for all your devices, lights and a Bluetooth speaker in the base."

My head was spinning with all this information. "Will it make me a cup of tea?" I asked in an attempt to process what he had just said.

"No, it doesn't have that capability yet. I think the designers assumed the end users would be more interested in having a cold beer!" he replied in all seriousness to my bizarre question – a true professional indeed!

Flummoxed by this, I decided I needed to retire from the situation and go somewhere to think through all this additional technology. Which of these 'enhancements' would be useful to us, or were they all just gimmicks to attract younger buyers?

Am I alone in hankering for simpler times, when household items just did what they were manufactured to do? When a sofa could be 'just a sofa', something comfy to sit on – that was its job – so why has it become so complicated?

6 FINANCIAL SHENANIGANS

Scammed and Still Sulking About It   **JW**

It was one of those little ads that pop up in your Facebook news feed that did for me. Somehow the unseen algorithms that litter the web with their 'bots capturing your every mouse click or keypress must have put two and two together and discovered my need for lightweight walking sandals. That made sense to me, I'd searched for walking sandals online. But I hadn't gone so far as to purchase anything and, anyway, how on earth did those insidious, invisible automata know that I have a craving for multi-coloured footwear?

It was late spring, last year. I was scrolling through multiple Facebook posts at speed to see what everyone was up to when the ad caught my eye. What was that I just saw? Fatefully, I checked myself before reading yet another post on a missing cat or a local garage sale and scrolled the screen back. A sale of Ecco sandals. And at under half the current retail price. Oh! And look at that pretty, multi-coloured shoe in the image. I'm your girl.

All caution forgotten in my eagerness, I clicked on the link. Those sandals really were just what I wanted. Now I'm no pushover, or so I thought and, regaining some sense, I prudently checked the images – they were definitely Ecco sandals. I'd eyed up similar models in their shoe shop in the centre of Bath but had jibbed at the price. The entire website for the "Ecco Sale" was presented well, functional and in good order with all the appropriate logos and typefaces. Not a misspelling in sight. Or so I thought, too distracted by the images of shoes, I didn't notice the tiny change in the URL.

I knew in my heart that the offer was likely to be too good to be true but temptation reared its ugly head. I really fancied those brightly coloured sandals and, at £23.99, they were a steal. But who was stealing from whom you rightly ask? In my arrogance I thought I would be able to spot if the transaction were to prove dodgy yet everything appeared normal, to the extent of being asked to register your email address and a password to set up an account. Nevertheless an alarm bell rang in my head when I got to the final checkout and was asked to pay in Australian dollars. I logged off immediately.

Yet I wanted those sandals so badly, it was such a good price for good quality shoes. I had a brainwave and Googled Ecco. They did indeed have branches in Australia and the shoes were made in Indonesia. It seemed entirely feasible that a factory outlet sale would expect to be paid in a local currency and I took the bait. Hook, line and sinker.

Delivery was promised within three weeks and I waited, waited patiently for a fourth yet with a icy feeling slowly sinking in my stomach all the while. I logged on, I could still see my order – the site was faultless (or so I thought, having still not spotted that tiny change in the URL). Another week went by. I researched the Ecco company complaints procedure and fired off an angry email about my missing shoes. I received a reply the same day. I was impressed with the speed of their customer service yet my heart sank at their reply. You can guess what it said.

I had known something was wrong but I still fell prey to the scammers. Infuriating!

The Scam   MR

It seems that almost every day

a scam of some sort comes my way

and yet it's not so long ago

it was a word I did not know.

But now I've almost come to dread

the word, and so instead

of looking forward to my post,

or emails, even texts, the most

I feel is a great relief.

If nothing is beyond belief,

nor can be trusted to be real

and not some awful dodgy deal.
Or worse than that some formal letter
claiming life would be much better
if I invest a thousand pounds
in bonds, whose interest knows no bounds.

My life will change they all declare
and soon I'll be a millionaire.
It's very easy to be scammed
when you are feeling 'not so grand'.
So never make a hasty choice,
or give your details to the voice
that's so persuasive, clear and bright –
they have your savings in their sight
and will do everything they can
to con you with their cunning scam.
So say "No thank you" loud and clear
or blow a 'raspberry' in their ear.
Hang up your phone – or leave it on
so they can't scam another one.
Then you're the winner, so to say,
you'll live to fight another day!

Just Chequing!   MP

I recently did a sponsored walk for charity. Distant friends sent me congratulations and cheques. They're the safest way to send money by post but dealing with them has proved less than simple. Not so very long ago I was able to walk to the bank in town, queue perhaps for five minutes if it was busy, hand over the cheques with a paying-in slip, and that was that.

All that has changed. The local branch of the bank has closed and been replaced by a mobile bank, scheduled to visit three times a week. That was a nuisance, but viable. There was a problem with getting a signal to connect the computers so various locations in the town centre were tried before settling on a regular spot. There is only room to deal with one person at a time and, of course, there is the question of privacy, so everyone has to queue outside in the street – hard luck if you have any mobility issues. And the queue is usually quite long because, since Covid, the frequency of the bank's visits has now been reduced even further.

I planned to take my cheques in on the next market day. Seeing no sign of the van when I arrived, I did my shopping in the hope that I was too early and the van had not yet arrived. Errands completed, there was still no van in its customary spot or anywhere else for that matter (I checked).

Frustrated, I went into the community Talking Café and mentioned my problem to someone there.

"Oh," she said, "It's only once a fortnight now. And they can't always get a signal so you can't be certain of dealing with anything at all."

All this leaves me having to drive nearly ten miles and pay for parking to deposit the cheques. So when they ask me "Can I help?" I shall tell them yet again that they can provide a better service to my local community. I'm not holding my breath.

Maths from the Bank   RC

"Two times twelve equals twenty."

That does not look right. Perhaps if it is presented numerically with a pound sign included it will be right.

"£2 x 12 = £20"

The above sum was part of a letter from my bank, about my annual bank charges, detailing that I had paid £2 per month charges on one account for a year. I made that £24 but the amount of money involved was too little to make a fuss about. I knew what had been paid and that was near enough. I snorted with derision but did nothing.

Twelve months later I opened two letters from the bank; identical letters received in the same post. I have long bemoaned poor interest rates and I saw this as a blatant waste of money: two lots of postage paid, the cost of printing the letters and someone's job to put them in envelopes and despatch them even if the folding and putting in envelopes is done mechanically. I don't know if it is but it still would have to be overseen and wage costs would be involved.

What were the letters about? Yes. Bank charges £2 per month for twelve months, total cost £20.

I wrote back correcting the maths and pointing out the need for better control to stop duplication of letters which wasted money: my money as I saw it for it is from customers that banks make their money though I did not put that in the letter.

A reply came. No apology or explanation, merely a statement.

"£2 per month for twelve months, total paid £24."

(I always ask for hard copies of any correspondence that comes in on line, in case you are wondering why anything came through the post.)

7 USE OF LANGUAGE

20th Century Gripes: a cinquain or two   JV

Cannot

abide misuse

of English grammar. No!

The split infinitive just grates.

It's wrong!

Neither

can I stand it

when "different to" is used

instead of "different from" A bad

mistake.

'Of' Importance   MP

There has been an incomprehensible change recently in the deployment of the word 'of'. The adverbial phrase 'out of' seems to have been replaced by the one word 'out'. For example, "I looked out the window." or "He ran out the door."

This can be explained by the 'law of least effort' that governs much of the development of language. For instance, it is much easier to say Beecham with its short vowel sounds than Beauchamp (Bowsharm) with its long ones and it is quicker to say 'can't' than 'cannot'. It is hard to argue against a new usage that follows the natural progression, however much I may dislike it. In fact it has become so pervasive that I have found myself 'looking out the window' on occasions, much to my dismay.

A more puzzling development is the contrasting lengthening of 'off' to 'off of'. I am unable to find any rationale for this. The extra word adds nothing to the meaning of the phrase. 'I jumped off of the bus' means exactly the same as 'I jumped off the bus'. There is perhaps a perverse analogy with such phrases as 'down to' and 'down from', but nothing that makes any sense. Whereas 'down from' and 'down to' indicate the direction of travel to an end point (I jumped down from the step', 'I am going down to the library'), 'off' indicates only a start point, in our example the bus. This is a new usage that children should definitely be warned off of!

Apostrophes (or should that be "apostrophe's") MP

Why are apostrophes always misplaced?
"Is'nt" **I've** seen (that's correct, it's not "Iv'e").
Am I just being old-fashioned, pedantic, strait-laced?
When **did** random punctuation arrive?

Potatoes are now commonly "potato's".
Yes, **sometimes** apostrophes come before "s",
but no one of sense would ever write "no'se" –
that clearly is stupid, in fact it's non'sen'se.

So wake up, you people, it's really not hard.
Use apostrophes to show things belong.
Shakespeare's sonnets were written by the bard
and I love to hear a **blackbird's** sweet song.

Sometimes an apostrophe's needed because
one letter or more is missing in speech,
"because" may be shortened to become **'cos**;
I have not one plum and **haven't** a peach.

It's really quite easy, just take some thought,
make **your** punctuation be as it ought.

Are We Even Speaking the Same Language? JW

I'm walking down the street with my teenage daughters one day and trying hard to pretend that I am not listening to their conversation.

"What do you think of Ollie then?" I hear one say.

"He's buff."

Now, even I know that she's not referring to the colour of the lad's skin for my son gave me a buff for Christmas last year. They're multipurpose stretchy tubes of patterned fabric, just the thing for protecting your face and ears from a cold wind but I'm still mystified. I promptly blow my cover.

"What about his buff?"

"Oh Mum, you know you shouldn't listen to other people's conversations."

Her elder sister relents and explains. Apparently buff now means fit-looking, it's a thing. I'm finding it hard to keep up. I've learned to be wary and double-check. If something's sick then it doesn't mean it's nauseating, exactly the opposite in fact. Wicked's similar, it's now something to aim for rather than to run from and I have learned not to panic if they mention dope, it only means that the thing being described is cool. To think that, not so many years ago, that phrase confused our own parents to whom, being cool only described the temperature.

I guess language will always continue to evolve and I will continue to have to try to keep up. Maybe one day I might finally work out what gaslighting means. However, there is most definitely an exception to this rule. "I'm good" is in no way a suitable or helpful reply to any of the following questions.

"I'm going into town, would you like a lift?"

"Have another roast potato?"

"How are you today?"

Yet I hear it all the time, from colleagues as well as my offspring. What is wrong with a polite "No thank you very much" or "I'm well, thank you for asking"? The English vocabulary is so rich, let's use it. Sadly though, I begin to wonder if George Orwell got it right and soon we will all be communicating via double-plus simple speak?

Responding to Politeness. It's Not an Age Thing
RC

A new pair of trousers was on the shopping list. I went to a well-known high street store only to find the kind I sought were no longer stocked. A duvet cover set caught my eye. I picked it up and went to pay. It was before nine thirty in the morning. There was one cashier at the end of a row of eight tills. I was the only customer in sight. I put the duvet set by her till.

"This side," she said indicating that I should have put it on the right, not the left. 'If she does not move that for me I shall not buy it,' I thought. She must have guessed from my expression that I was not happy.

"Oh very well then," she said moving the item to the side of the till where she wanted it and plonking it down.

I duly paid and left the store.

I recounted my experience to a son who said.

"That's how it is now, Mum. You're just old fashioned. You need to move with the times."

'If there are no customers, she won't have a job,' I thought but said no more.

A grandson, aged twenty five, shops in a gentlemen's outfitters in the market town where he lives. Their stock, when it comes to style, has moved with the times. It sells brands he likes, Barbour and Loake for example. The ambience of the shop has not changed in fifty years. It is as it was when his grandfather shopped there. I asked why he likes that particular shop.

"I like the service," he said. "I am greeted with a polite. 'Can I help you?' followed by 'If you care to come this way' and I am led to the area I need. I'm not looking to be called 'Sir' but sometimes they say 'Can I help you, Sir?' I nearly always get what I want. They are helpful, welcoming and so polite. I like it."

So it's not just me!

8 CAUTIONARY VERSES FOR TWENTY-FIRST CENTURY CHILDREN

Not So Little Jimmy   **JW**

Little Jimmy was a podgy child,
his fat cheeks dimpled when he smiled.
His mother thought the world of him
but the doctors said to our Jim.
If you eat too many sweeties
you'll end up with diabetes.
Excess lemonade and colas
means you'll be obese and toeless.
But Jimmy didn't stop to think

and gulped down yet more fizzy drink.
I'm afraid Jimmy didn't stop
until one day he just went pop!
Yet should we blame the child you ask?
Taking the producers to task
would make more sense for it's they that
load their goods with sugars and fat.

Johnny Glued to His Phone   MP

Johnny, when just a little lad,
would nearly drive his parents mad.
He wouldn't play or read, just moan,
until the day he got a phone.

He did not like to watch TV.
He said "It's for the family!
I can't be bothered with all that –
the goggle box is so old hat."

When reading friends' posts on TikTok,
he always failed to watch the clock,
which made him very late for school.
He didn't care, thought he was cool.

Some boys would waste time on MineCraft.
"Creating things," he said, "is daft!
Who wants to make cows out of bricks
and then watch them performing tricks?"

His mother quite despaired of him.
So did his friends, who thought him dim.
One day he found himself alone –
his only friend was just a phone.

So if you want to have a life,
have friends and kids, a loving wife,
don't spend too much time, boys, online.
Life is out there, go, you'll be fine!

Music to Die For?   CN

Amy, when you walk down the streets,
try to resist list'ning to beats.
Don't have a hindrance in each ear,
noises round you, you just won't hear.
No awareness of the dangers,
you won't hear approaching strangers.
And what about the speeding bike?
In painful moments it might strike
you wandering across the road
from the shop to your own abode.
You won't hear the car beep its horn
and then your family will mourn.
Killed by your love of melodies?
No! Understand my advice please –
Leave your love of music at home
be aware of sounds when you roam.

AND ADULTS TOO?

Should We Keep Taking the Tablets?   MR

The chief defect with Meg's iPad
was that if often drove her mad.
Her emails sometimes disappeared.
Which seemed to her to be so weird
when what she did was just the same,
text writ, keys tapped and sent by name
to those awaiting her new prose...
But where it goes to no-one knows
and Meg sits wondering what they thought
as no response is ever brought.
What causes even more frustration,
anger and long rumination
is that laptop, watch and phone
have shown that they are also prone
to freeze, delete, install, shut down.
Whilst she can only sit and frown
and wonder if her age belies
the obvious before her eyes.
Perhaps it's time to think again
And trust her faithful fountain pen?!

The Right Way Up?   JV

Mary thought she'd go quite posher
Buying, new, a smart dishwasher
No more washing up! How thrilling!
Now she needs to learn (God willing)
how to load it up and stack it,
put in tablet, salt from packet.
(All instructions overrated.)
Throw in knives with blades serrated
sticking upwards in the basket.
(Oh dear, Mary, you have asked it.)
Door left open, chucked in saucers,
plates and spoons from all the courses.
Then she slipped and hit her head-oh!
Knives did pierce her skull. And dead-oh.
Lesson learned (and do not frown),
always put the knives blades down.

Jane Who Fell Prey to a Phisher   JW

Jane was Clever or so she thought.
But her quick thinking came to Naught
the miserable day that Greed
overrode her desire to read
the Small Print on a shop's website.
To check the contract's watertight.

Tempted by a phishing email,
Jane bought boots in an online sale.
The Boots themselves never arrived
yet her Bank Account was deprived
of Ten times the expected sum
leaving Jane deeply Shocked and Glum.

A Decimal Point had been moved.
Loving a bargain, she'd approved
the sale without a careful check.
She'd been truly Fleeced by hi-tech
robbers who, wise to Women's ways,
leave them Poorer and somewhat dazed.

Lastly, when she went to Complain,
Jane was left feeling Numb again.
Her bank account had Disappeared.
Her Bank Manager laughed, he feared
she'd Lost the lot. Jane's now Begging,
all for want of Double Checking.

Rosemarie's Aunt   RC

My poor old aunt was such a jerk,
she could not make her mobile work.
"Slide that bit up," at her I'd shout.
"Why can't you see what it's about?"

She smiled and said, "The day will come.
Technology will strike you dumb."
Today with friends I laugh or groan
whilst in a room quite on my own.

A selfie on my 'phone I click.
A Satnav finds a route that's quick.
I talk to robots on the 'phone.
Hide from a neighbour's nosy drone.

Get cash from just outside the bank.
Card payment fills my fuel tank.
My doctor will give me a ring.
It seems a visit's not the thing.

My in-box email gets quite clogged,
appointments, bills, they all are logged.
Enough's enough. Today I'll go
and idly watch the river flow.

But...   MP

They tell me that Bitcoin's the thing
if you fancy a financial fling.
I've a tanner or two –
I'm sure those will do,
but what sort of return will they bring?

9 IN A FANTASY WORLD

Device of My Dreams   **MP**

For my grandmother, the unimaginable luxury would have been my laptop, for my mother it would have been my mobile phone. For me it is the 'UniRecycle' – a robot which deals with all the household recycling.

Imagine simply putting all waste into a hole in the wall in the kitchen – no fuss, no mess, no time at all. Vacuum suction takes the waste through a tube and into a sorting device standing outside by the wall. In the reception area of the device, the type of waste is identified and despatched to the appropriate internal bin.

On collection day, the UniRecycle first seals and disconnects the tube, then it propels itself to the kerbside ready to be emptied. When empty, it returns to its position, connects its cleaner pipe to an outside tap and enters a cleaning phase where water is circulated through the bins and down into a nearby drain. Hot air is then blown through to dry out the bins. Finally, they are sanitised by ultra-violet light, the cleaner pipe is disconnected and the feeder tube reconnected. The device is now ready for use again.

The UniRecycle would need to be programmable to accommodate the differences in recycling rules between Local Authorities. For instance, mine allows plastics and tins to be collected in the same container, where others require these to be separated. Similarly, it would be necessary to program the frequency of collection of certain types of waste as well as the collection days and times for the Local Authority area. Naturally an over-ride would be necessary to allow for public holiday variations.

Whilst these devices were rare, operatives would still be needed to load the waste into the Council trucks. However, future development would allow for automatic loading of the vehicle at the touch of a button.

A UniRecyle would save me so much time and effort. I would no longer need to remember what gets collected on which week. I would not even have to remember which day of the week it was.

I wish…

Wishful Thinking   JW

For me the ultimate technological gadget would be a 'dust zapper'. I hate dusting, it's so pointless. Every week or so you spend a not inconsiderable amount of time in, say, your front room carefully dusting the windowsills, the dresser, the sideboard, the mantelpiece, the vases on the mantelpiece. Even your sunglasses that have been missing for months and you've finally found hiding behind a vase on the mantelpiece. Should you be so lucky as to own a piano it needs a thorough wipe over, all the way down to the pedals. How do piano pedals get so dusty? It's one of the mysteries of life. Then it's the turn of the picture frames and finally, the skirting. Yet on the very same day, in the evening sun, sure as eggs are eggs, the room will be starting to look dusty again.

My dust zapper would be a lightweight, narrow blade, maybe two to three feet long and glowing with blue light along the lines of the light sabres from the Star Wars movies. The hilt would fit my hand like a glove with its on-off switch located beneath my thumb. The guard would both protect my hand as I brandished the zapper to electrostatically attract all the dust in the room and act as a power source for the blade. The dust collection bag would clip to your sword arm so you would know to empty it as soon as its weight was noticeable.

Chanelling my inner Darth Vadar, I would wield the zapper like a light sabre as I entered the front room 'en garde' as if I were a fencer, advancing with front foot first then back. With a flourish I would wave the dust zapper's column of light over the sideboard, then again, through the objects on the mantelpiece and finally pirouette to step and lunge at the old piano. Within seconds every particle of dust in sight will have been drawn into the collector.

This would be so much fun that I would voluntarily do every room in the house each week. The source of power would be an issue but that's another story.

"Beam Me Up! Scotty"   CN

I guess that everyone of my generation refers back to the original series of 'Star Trek' when considering the progress of new technologies – or is it just me?

We were in awe at the ease with which the crew members could communicate with each other using hand held devices, never thinking that such a thing would be possible in our lifetime. Look where we are today.

Perhaps the technology that I hoped would be developed was the intriguing process of teleportation, although I did wonder if it would be very painful having all the cells in your body dematerialised and then materialised again in such quick time.

Imagine the advantages of being able to teleport to anywhere on the planet – what a great way to solve the climate change issue? If it was possible to move people and things to anywhere else in the world without the need to put them on fuel guzzling planes, trains and automobiles – many of our problems would be solved.

No more checking in at airports, although I suppose there would have to be transport hubs of some sort – people wouldn't be able to disappear and suddenly reappear at another distant point without scheduling – imagine the chaos!

What would happen if your cells bumped into the cells of someone, or something else, whilst miraculously floating through the airwaves? You might end up as part of another person or thing. Obviously, there would have to be strict regulations to stop that happening.

In many ways, it seems too difficult to develop teleportation as an actual thing, but then again ALL technologies must have seemed impossible at some stage during their invention process. Perhaps Elon Musk should be working on this solution to the world's problems, rather than looking at setting up bases on the moon or Mars – they seem far-fetched too!

I will have to leave the details to the scientists, I have my fingers crossed there is a boffin, in a laboratory somewhere, working on this right now!

A Surprisingly Happy Compromise   MR

It had been a very difficult conversation – one that Hilary had been dreading, but had also known that it was inevitable now that her sight had almost gone. She had found herself thinking back to the time forty years ago when she had taken the lead in a similar talk with her father. Her mother could no longer care for him at home. They didn't want an ever-changing parade of carers and the only realistic alternative was a care home. He had hated the very idea, and would only consider it if her mother would go in with him. The expression on her mother's face had said it all. Much as she loved him and wanted the best for him, her needs were very different and did not include being 'incarcerated' as she saw it. It had been a very traumatic time for everyone.

As the pros and cons of her own future were rehearsed; the lack of available carers and the unlikelihood of finding a regular person who would come several times a day, every day; the astronomical costs of a care home were deliberated. Her younger son – the technological wizard – had tentatively suggested an alternative that no-one else had even considered.

"You know Mum, there maybe IS a way that you could stay here, in your own home. There's a trial being conducted locally and I reckon you might well meet their criteria for acceptance."

"Tell me more" she said "Anything is worth considering if I could stay in this house with my own things around me, and the cat on my lap."

"Well, if you were successful in joining the trial you would be allocated a full time resident 'carer' for the rest of your life. There is an upfront cost of £5000 plus a monthly payment of £350 which includes the rental of any additional equipment that the 'carer' might need."

"That sounds affordable" she said "When could she start? – I'm assuming we're talking about a woman. Could I meet her first, to be sure that she would fit in with me and that we'd get on?"

"That won't be a problem" Ben said "They would send a male or a female – whichever you prefer and would make certain that your personalities and interests matched."

And so it was agreed that they would apply to be part of the trial and would hopefully be matched with a 'carer' very soon.

Roberta arrived a few weeks later. Ben had taken a day off work to see her safely installed in her new home and to ensure that everything was running smoothly. He went through the programme of what needed to happen throughout the day and overnight, making sure that all the instructions were clear. Hilary seemed quite happy with her new companion and Roberta was content to listen and respond to her questions, comments and requests, moving around the house quietly and efficiently, leaving everything clean and tidy and in its proper place. Hilary was surprisingly at ease with Roberta and Ben felt confident in leaving them together, promising that either he or his wife would pop in each day to check that all was well.

Four incident free weeks later, Ben arrived to find all was quiet and peaceful, the house was looking immaculate and his mother was full of smiles and tales to tell. Roberta was having a rest – no doubt re-charging her batteries after a busy morning cleaning and cooking. It seemed like a good time to have a chat with his Mum and see how she was feeling about her live-in carer.

"So tell me, Mum" he said "how is it going? Did we make the right decision? Are you happy with Roberta? Is there anything that we need to change?"

"Oh no, dear", Roberta is the perfect companion. She does anything I ask her to without ever complaining. She only speaks when spoken to, unless she has a question to ask or something to tell me. She will read to me for hours if I want her to, and seems to know just the sort of books I enjoy. I've no idea how she manages to get hold of them so quickly. She's much better than the television, which in any case is only a blur now. I'm a bit worried about her though. I don't think she's eating enough. Her fingers are very bony and she will never sit and have a cuppa and piece of cake with me. I don't want her to get sick – I would miss having her around. The only thing is that the cat doesn't seem too sure about her, but I expect that will pass in time."

When Ben returned home that evening and was filling his wife in on his visit he sighed and said. "I've been wondering for a while whether Mum's sight is even worse than we thought, but after our chat today I realised that it is not only her sight that has gone. She clearly has no idea that Roberta is a robot! Still, she is happy and well looked after. If she can pass the rest of her allotted time in her own home with all her treasures around her, then there is a great deal to be said for the wonders of AI.

10 AND FINALLY, THE GOOD NEWS

Paying for Parking **RC**

Well, there is a cause for celebration, or there was in my case when I succeeded in paying to park my car using my debit card. After the trauma of new credit card registration which involved multiple mechanical voices and then the need to find my mobile phone in a hurry for the verification plus, of course, glasses to read the bank's text, I excused myself mentally by using age as an excuse. (I avoid the word dementia.)

Recently I had to go to the solicitor. My walking is poor and I can only manage a short distance. It was imperative that I use the nearest carpark. On arrival I found it only took cards and there was no option to use cash. Following the instructions on the screen, which thankfully were very clear, I pressed the right buttons to set time needed then held the card in front of the icon displayed. There was a bleep so it had worked. I got a ticket to put in the car and also asked for a receipt which duly dropped out.

It was easier than using cash. I was impressed. I must try it again.

The pay centres in the town give options for card or cash and, I believe, payment by 'phone though I am not ready for that last challenge. At every step on the way to the solicitor I told myself how clever I was. I had paid for parking using a card. There is hope for the old girl yet.

My Big Success   JV

Our twenty-first century gripes are mostly IT related because we did not grow up with computers, had little or no instruction in the use of them and have spent our latter years endeavouring to get a grip on what is a bewildering array of technology in order to be able to operate life online.

We all have stories of disasters – some amusing, some not so funny. However, I have recently had a success of which I am extremely proud.

Being over 70, I need to renew my driving licence every three years. Failure to do so would mean either a refusal to renew or taking another driving test – the criteria for passing which at such an advanced age is reputed to be tougher than ever was the original – especially as there is now a written test as well. Triennial paranoia and panic about renewal, understandably, thus sets in.

My current licence was due to expire at the end of January 2023. One is able to renew not more than 90 days in advance so I calculated that would be Bonfire Night and not before. I left my current licence lying about in the kitchen for weeks so as to remind myself about it.

The 5th November dawned. In trepidation I Googled "renewal of UK driving licences for those over 70" or something similar and was directed to an online form. Pages of questions had to be answered. One completed one page at a time and then pressed "Continue" for the next page. One needed one's NHI number, the number of one's current licence and one's passport number. One is not warned in advance of the need for these so there was a seven minute delay while I left the page opened in order to locate my passport – itself fairly recently renewed (but not online). I was pleased that the site remained open while I looked for the passport and not closed as "time expired" as is usually the case.

There was another hiccup when asked if one needed corrective lenses in order to read a number plate so many yards away. I have worn glasses for everything for the last 30 years and have not driven without them for decades so I really do not know if I can see a number plate so many yards way without them so answered "Yes". The site took a while to process this information and I was not allowed to continue. Uh huh! I thought! Bad answer! Just as I thought I would change the answer, the site came alive again and allowed me to go to the next page. This was getting to be a bit like "Big Brother is watching you" – the site was clearly thinking as each answer was made – rather unnerving I felt!

Then, horror of horrors, the website told me I needed to have a new photo of myself. If there is one thing quite beyond my capabilities it is uploading any document or picture into anything so my efforts so far seemed doomed. To my surprise however, the site asked me if I would like DVLA to use the same photo as had been used in my recently renewed passport to which I gratefully said yes please. How did the site know my passport had recently been renewed with a new photo of myself? Had it been checking while I was online? Was there a site gremlin feverishly working away behind the scenes?

Anyway, that seemed to be it and I was told I would have a new licence in about six weeks' time. In the meantime, I was authorised to drive even if, as I had to promise I would, I had cut up my current licence and returned it to DVLA.

Two days later my new licence arrived complete with the same new photo as is in my passport and with my usual signature. Amazing! I have been gloating ever since with my successful on line achievement! It has so gone to my head that I may well try something else on line. You never know.

Technology that Keeps Me Sane   RC

From the news headline that the first heart transplant had taken place to today, the impact of technology on our lives has been and still is, amazing, overwhelming. There are not enough forceful adjectives to describe it. It is embedded in our lives. Multi-programs on washing machines, medicines, information from blood tests, vaccines, mobile phones that can detect an irregular heart beat or read blood sugar levels, gadgets that tell us how far we have walked, smart meters in the kitchen, microwave ovens, the list goes on.

The apps for which I am most grateful include Office 365 and Zoom. It all began during Lock Down and the Covid scare. I live alone and was very isolated. Yes, a relative shopped for me and life was sustained but the days were long and lonely. Office 365 and the associated apps were a life-line for it was possible to send and receive messages. My use has only increased since.

The grandchildren, all in their twenties, send me photos from their lives, of shooting to winning dog shows, a newly purchased first home to ski-ing or playing American Football. One sends me recipes, another, pictures of her travels in the Far East. A godson has moved to New Zealand. I have photos of his newly built house.

I feel very much part of their lives thanks to technology. In return I send photos of my garden or attach a poem that I have written. Very tame compared to the lives they lead.

Other information and invitations arrive by email when friends are keeping me 'in the loop' and settling details of outings. They also send holiday snaps. Friends from Norway, the USA, Australia and New Zealand, keep in touch via email. It is unlikely that I shall meet up with my Norwegian friend of fifty years again. She sends photos of her great grandchildren. We are well in touch.

News comes from Ann in Sydney. She had not met the term 'ping meal'. It amused her. Her reply was full of chuckles. She had latched on to the term which she got from me via email.

An ex-colleague, now living in Louisiana, writes of her travels.

I no longer drive after dark and I can join RSPB lectures through online video during the winter. Zoom enables me to attend a writing group. Both the RSPB and the BTO send regular news letters by email.

A joy at Christmas is to have the family get together using Microsoft Teams. Three, four or more households are linked. We can all chat and see each other. A quiz is set for us all. It is very special. If we cannot be together this is the next best thing.

The Hole-In-The-Wall   MP

I needed some cash to go to the shops –
nothing special, just groceries and such –
so I went and stood in the wind and the rain
at our local hole-in-the-wall.

"Please insert your card and enter your PIN.
What service do you want today?"
"Just give me some cash and receipt, "I replied
to that courteous hole-in-the-wall.

"How much would you like? To help you decide
I'll give you some options to choose:
ten, twenty or fifty, a hundred?" enquired
that so-helpful hole-in-the-wall.

Now I had a dilemma – none of these fit the bill,
but lucky for me there was more;
one button said 'Other amount', which I pressed.
A convenient hole-in-the-wall.

"Please enter amount", so I typed in a six
then a five, with all fingers crossed tight.
A long pause ensued before the reply
from the thoughtful hole-in-the-wall.

"I can't do that sum". My heart sank, but no,
the machine was not finished just yet.
"Sixty thousand, seven hundred's my offer. OK?"
said that generous hole-in-the-wall.

I thought of the sunshine in Monte or Spain,
of the ruins in Pompeii and Rome,
then I thought of the people who'd come and then find
just an empty hole-in-the-wall.

I thought of my bank account – it would see red
if I took out the money and ran!
It was clear this machine had a GSOH –
a surprising hole-in-the-wall.

I cancelled the lot and then started again,
with a smile on my face, it is true.
What a helpful, generous, truly surprising,
wonderful hole-in-the-wall!

When Technology Works   JV

It was a bright sunny day at the end of July 2023. My husband and I, our two adult daughters and their respective labradoodles had been for a long walk on Minchinhampton Common. We had lunched in a local hostelry and at 3.00pm in the afternoon were heading home in the trusted Volvo Estate. Dogs were in the boot, daughters strapped in the back seats, snoozing, me in the passenger seat, also snoozing. The snooziness of the three of us was on account of having each imbibed several glasses of wine at lunch. My husband was driving and had just had a ginger beer.

We were on the home straight on Welsh Way having just been through Honeycomb Leaze, a hamlet only a quarter of a mile from our cottage. I awoke suddenly to find the car at a 45 degree angle in a deep ditch and what looked like smoke rising in front of me. "Get the dogs out" I yelled believing the car to be on fire and in immediate danger of exploding. Both girls got out of the back and opened the boot to get the dogs out. I opened the passenger seat and climbed out onto a grass verge. Scarily, my husband appeared to be trapped in the driver's seat which was now at the bottom of the ditch but the girls managed to haul him out. None of us was hurt in the slightest.

"What happened?" we all cried. My husband had no idea. One minute he had been driving on the road and the next minute he was not. We shall never know why. He simply does not remember and the rest of us were asleep. He has had medical tests since, all of which were negative and gave no clue as to the possible cause. It was fortunate there were no trees on that bit of the road and nothing was coming the other way

My elder daughter had recently acquired a brand new smart phone. Without her doing anything at all, it knew we had been in an accident and had automatically rung the emergency services. The police came, breathalysed my husband who was zero rated and said we were lucky to have been in a Volvo. He drove my husband and myself home leaving the girls and the dogs to walk themselves back the few hundred yards to the cottage.

The seat belts had automatically tightened on impact; the airbags had exploded as they should have done and the billowing dust from them had been what I had thought was smoke. The front of the car had crumpled as it was designed to do leaving the steel skeleton of the car intact. The automatic brakes had brought us to a halt without my husband having to apply them and all in all the emergency functions had all faultlessly come into operation. My daughter's phone had of its own accord summoned both the police and an ambulance – the latter fortunately not being required and, for once, I was immensely grateful for modern technology.

Afterthought   RC

If this were panto I'd be Widow Twanky in conversation with Prince Charming who, in turn, will be joined by the audience.

Widow Twanky: I've cracked technology.

Prince Charming and the audience: Oh no you haven't.

Widow Twanky: Oh yes I have.

Prince Charming and the audience: Oh no you haven't.

Unfortunately Prince Charming is right. A while back I was going, with a group, birdwatching. I arrived late. I paid for parking and got a ticket for the dashboard. The wind caught it and it was blown away. Embarrassed to keep everyone waiting I bought another and successfully displayed it as per the instructions on the pay machine. Yes a ticket must be displayed.

Time moved on. In Cirencester I parked in a car park that only took payment by debit card. All straightforward. I got the required ticket and a receipt. I displayed the ticket.

Widow Twanky. I've cracked technology.

Prince Charming: Oh no you haven't.

This week I met a grandson for lunch. He drove. I gave him change for the parking meter. There was a coin jammed so he took out his 'phone, photographed his number plate and paid for three hours parking.

"You've not displayed a ticket," I said.

"I don't have to. The traffic warden will take a snap of my number plate and know I have paid."

Two days later I met three friends for lunch.

Widow Twanky: I do like eating out.

Prince Charming: Oh yes she does!

One friend gave me a lift. Another arrived late. Time sped by. "Excuse me," said one, "I'll have to get my phone out to add more parking time. I only paid for two hours." She got out her phone. No signal so she went into the road. "All done," she said as she sat down.

Widow Twanky: I've not cracked this technology stuff.

Prince Charming; No, she has not.

Not only can you pay to park by phone, no ticket to display and you can remotely add on more time. So clever. I'm gobsmacked!

The Fairford u3a Creative Writing Group meets weekly on Friday mornings during term time. We use Zoom a lot but try to ensure we meet up face to face at least monthly. There is more information at https://fairfordu3a.uk/ should you wish to join us. You would be very welcome.

Printed in Great Britain
by Amazon

30556013R00066